{ The Little Book of Loony Laws }

{ The Little Book of Loony laws }

Christine Green

ILLUSTRATED BY

Besley

www.vitalspark.co.uk

The Vital Spark is an imprint of
Neil Wilson Publishing Ltd
303a The Pentagon Centre
36 Washington Street
GLASGOW G3 8AZ

Tel: 0141-221-1117
Fax: 0141-221-5363
E-mail: info@nwp.sol.co.uk
http://www.nwp.co.uk

A catalogue record for this book is
available from the British Library.

ISBN 1-903238-61-7

Typeset in Slimbach
Designed by Mark Blackadder

Printed and bound in Poland

Contents

Introduction 7

Introduction

The legal system worldwide is a Pandora's box of fascinating and frequently mind-boggling laws created by learned men and women to protect you, the supposedly 'ordinary person on top of the Clapham omnibus'. These laws can often take months, even years to reach the statute books and some never even make it there and so remain destined to the wastepaper bin. Yet flicking through the archives of ancient chronicles it is amazing to find some of the loony laws that have actually been passed and survived.

The famous lexicographer, Samuel Johnson once wrote, 'The law is the last result of human wisdom acting upon human experience for the benefit of the public.' Perhaps some of his moral philosophy leaves a lot to be desired.

Flicking through these archaic laws it would seem that many were created to entertain and amuse although there must have been some initial reasoning behind them in the first place. Take for example the law in Lawrence, Kansas that bans anyone from carrying bees in their hat or the law in Scotland that states that if a stranger should knock on your door and require the use of your commode then you must allow them to enter.

And some laws are so ridiculous it takes a lot to believe they actually ever made it to paper; after all who would even contemplate instigating a law that made it illegal to land a flying saucer in the vineyards of France!

This wee book is a compilation from the sublime to the cor blimey, the bizarre, even wacky laws that have been gathered from around the world from various sources and all destined to give the reader something to smile about. Some of the laws are still standing on the statute books, albeit never enforced, whilst others have been repealed. But there is one thing you can be assured about … they are genuine and quite, quite loony!

Christine Green

In Australia ...

... although not permitted to smoke cigarettes children can legally purchase them.

... if a light bulb goes out then only fully licensed electricians are allowed to change it. Otherwise a fine of 10 dollars will be charged.

... many years ago a law was passed making it illegal for anyone to walk the streets wearing black clothes, felt shoes and black shoe polish on their face as the authorities regarded all three items as being the costume of a cat burglar.

… the Dieri tribe has strict (and confusing) laws regarding whom one can marry. For example, a man can legally marry his mother's mother's brother's daughter's daughter. He can also marry his mother's father's sister's daughter's daughter.

… 'Lollipop Ladies' are only funded by the Transport Department if 45 or more children use the crossing each day unaided by either parents or guardians. Should the 'Lollipop Lady' be helped to do her job then her funding can be withdrawn.

… when going outdoors, cats in the town of Longhorn must wear three little bells on their collars to warn birds of their approach.

… according to the Telecommunications Act 1991 and under the Australian Communications Authority (ACA) legislation, a modem is not allowed to connect on the first ring. If it does then the ACA permit is invalid and the operator is fined.

… in Victoria it is illegal to wear 'hot pink pants' after 12 noon on a Saturday.

In Bermuda …

… it is illegal to drive at over 20mph.

… tourists are banned from hiring cars and may only travel by moped, bus or taxi.

10

... it is not permitted to take a suitcase on a public bus.

... women must not wear skirts shorter than 8 inches (20cm) above the knee in public places.

... neither are women permitted to wear halter neck tops in public places.

... it is illegal to drive a car or ride a bike without a shirt on.

... a radio must be audible no more than 16 feet (4.88 metres) from a car.

... only one car is allowed per household.

... cars cannot be wider than 67 inches (1.7 metres) or longer than 169 inches (4.30 metres).

... you may has many motorbikes as you wish, as long as the engine size is no bigger than 150cc.

In Bolivia ...

... in Santa Cruz, it is illegal for a man to have sex with a woman and her daughter at the same time.

...in Santa Cruz, although a woman can legally be a prostitute it is illegal for her to solicit customers on the street or in any public place.

… women are legally prohibited from drinking more than one glass of wine in bars and restaurants, because it is thought to weaken them sexually and make them easy prey for male advances. Any woman who breaks the law can expect a hefty fine and it is also seen as grounds for divorce.

In Brazil …

… in the Tupie tribe a woman must be faithful to her husband, yet he is allowed as many mistresses as he can afford.

… in Sorocaba, passionate kissing in public places is illegal.

... the censorship laws in Brazil are very strict, with explicit guidelines governing pornography. No pictures of nude couples, women dressed in bikinis or short shorts, or photographs even suggesting sexual activity are allowed in any publication. No more than one bare female breast may be legally shown on any given page of a magazine, newspaper, book or any other publication.

In Canada ...

... a law was passed that any debts higher than 25 cents could not be paid with pennies.

... when raining in Nova Scotia a person is not allowed to water his or her lawn.

... until 1998 guests staying at the Queen Elizabeth Hotel, Montreal, had their horses fed for free by the hotel.

... in Toronto it was illegal for anyone to ride a streetcar on a Sunday after having eaten garlic.

... the government imposed a statute which insisted that margarine be coloured dark vermilion, in response to complaints from local dairy lobbyists. They claimed that margarine was beginning to resemble butter and that the only way to differentiate it was to change the colour and make it unattractive to the consumer. After a negative response to the vermilion spread, the colour finally emerged as a pallid, almost white colourless margarine.

... legislation decreed that when it snows in Oshawa it is the sole responsibility of the homeowners to clear the public sidewalks. If the sidewalks aren't cleaned within 24 hours after a snowfall, city workers will clean it but the cost will be placed on the homeowners' tax bill.

... as recently as April 2000 it was a law in Canada that the Government would pay a bounty for all Indian scalps brought in.

... motorists living in Montreal may not wash their car in the street, nor may they park their car in such a way as it obstructs their own driveway.

... it is illegal to swear in French in Montreal, although there are no restrictions on doing so in English.

... In Uxbridge residents are not allowed to have an internet connection faster than 56k.

... a bill passed in 1976 ordered that all business signs in the province of Quebec must be written in French. Should the business operator wish to have English on the sign then the French wording should be written at least double the size of the English.

... urinating or spitting on the streets of Montreal was a punishable offence with a fine of over 100 Canadian dollars.

... the law of Etobicoke states that anyone taking a bath must have no more than 3.5 inches of water in a bathtub before they enter it.

… in Alberta you cannot use dice to play the game of craps.

… although the speed limit in Ontario is 80kph for motorcars, cyclists have the right of way.

… in Saskatchewan it is illegal to watch exotic dancers

In Chile …

… in Cautin Province it is illegal for any home or public building to exhibit *Playboy* centrefolds and other such material, as it is thought to be far more worthwhile to admire a beautiful landscape than a photograph of a naked woman.

… it is illegal in Valparaiso for a man to take a woman who has committed adultery for his bride.

…divorce does not exist. Wealthy couples wishing to separate may have the marriage dissolved through a process with a sympathetic judge in which the couple claim that their address does not match that on the marriage certificate.

In China …

… according to Article 40 of the Beijing Traffic Laws, drivers of motor vehicles who stop at pedestrian crossings are likely to receive a warning or a fine.

… because the country is so heavily populated families are only allowed to have one child.

… a law existed which banned any man from looking at the naked feet of another man's wife. The law did not extend to other parts of the female anatomy.

… in order to go to college you must be 'intelligent'.

… women are prohibited from walking around a hotel room naked. The only place where she may be unclad is in the privacy of her bathroom.

… in Beijing it is illegal for a foreigner to take a Chinese woman to his hotel room for sex.

In Denmark …

… there is a penalty of 20kr for anyone who fails to report the death of a person to the authorities.

… it is illegal to start a car if there is anyone underneath.

… restaurants may not charge for water unless it is accompanied by items such as ice or a slice of lemon.

… if a horse-drawn carriage is trying to pass a car and the horse becomes uneasy the driver is required to pull over and if necessary, cover the car from the horse's view.

In Ecuador ...

... a young bride can be returned to her parents if her husband discovers she is not a virgin on their wedding night.

... a woman may legally dance in public wearing nothing more than a piece of gauze covering her belly button.

In Egypt ...

... 6,000 years ago rape was punishable with castration. A woman found guilty of adultery would find herself without a nose, the thinking being that without a nose it would be more difficult for her to find someone to share in her adulterous ways.

... whenever a woman was convicted of a crime in ancient Egypt, her children were also generally punished.

... taking photographs or using binoculars close to a government or military installation is banned – penalties may well incur a prison sentence.

... and just as in Ecuador a law banned women from belly dancing unless their navel was covered with a piece of gauze.

In El Salvador ...

... 'any married woman who lies with a man who is not her husband' can receive a fine and a six-year term in prison.

... in Santa Ana, having sex with a relative is a serious offence. The violators are either exiled or hanged.

In Finland ...

... the Helsinki Police do not issue parking tickets to motorists who illegally park, but instead deflate their car tyres.

... to get married, the law stipulates that both the man and woman are able to read.

... at one time Donald Duck comics were banned because Donald didn't wear any pants.

...if you get fined for speeding or some other crime then the amount you are requested to pay to the courts relates to your personal financial position. So the richer you are, the more you pay.

In France ...

... kissing on French railways is illegal.

... there used to be a law that parents had to take their children's names from an official government list.

... provided that she was willing to join the opera, an 18th-century prostitute could be spared punishment.

... one punishment for an adulterous wife in medieval France was to make her chase a chicken through town, naked.

... the sale of dolls with alien faces is banned. All dolls must have human faces.

... no pig owner may call his or her pig Napoleon.

… in Antibes, it is illegal to take photographs of French police officers or police vehicles, even if they are just in the background.

… a law was passed making it illegal for anyone to stare at the mayor of Paris.

… it is illegal to land a flying saucer in the vineyards of France.

Sod the dent in your spaceship - just look what it's done to my Chablis!

In Germany ...

... all office workers must have a view of the sky, however small.

... it is illegal to wear a mask.

... a pillow is regarded as being a 'passive weapon'.

… a beer purity law was passed in 1516. The Reinheitsgebot, the Bavarian Purity Law, states that beer must be made with only malted grains, water and hops. Many people believe it mentions yeast but it doesn't – yeast was first mentioned in a Munich regulation in 1551.

In Great Britain …

… it is illegal for a Member of Parliament to enter the House of Commons wearing a full suit of armour.

… the slaughtering or dressing of cattle in the streets is illegal, unless the aforementioned animal has been recently run over by the person who is doing the slaughtering or dressing.

… in London it is illegal to drive a car without sitting in the front seat.

... a pregnant woman can legally urinate anywhere she wants to, including in a policeman's helmet.

... anyone caught sticking chewing gum to the underside of a seat on the upper deck of a bus can be detained in custody for 24 hours if they are caught.

... it is illegal to disturb any animals grazing on the Victoria Embankment Gardens, Shepherd's Bush Common or any other open space in London.

... in the Middle Ages if any person was found breaking a boiled egg at the pointed end their punishment was a day and a night in the village stocks.

... in Liverpool it is illegal for a woman to be topless in public unless she is employed as a clerk in a tropical fish store.

... in Scotland, if a stranger should knock on your door and require the use of your commode then you must allow them to enter.

... until 1998 there was a law in which interfering with the monarch's mail or sleeping with the consort of the monarch carried the maximum penalty of death by hanging.

... there was once a law that every city council member in Manchester had to attend church each Sunday.

... in Somerset it was once ordained that people were not to wear the same clothes on Sunday as they did during the rest of the week.

... in Upton upon Severn it is illegal for married couples to live in a discarded bus.

In Greece ...

... Greece has banned all forms of computer entertainment including consoles, arcades and PC games in the home. People have been fined a great deal of money for owning Gameboys and if anyone is caught playing online chess in a cyber café, then the café is closed down.

... a driver's licence can be revoked if the driver is deemed poorly dressed or even appears to be unwashed.

... it is illegal to take photographs at airports and at military and airforce installations.

... in Athens, in the 6th century, legislator Solon passed a law which allowed fathers to sell their fornicating daughters into slavery.

In Guinea ...

... it is illegal to give the name 'Monica' to a baby.

In Iceland ...

... anybody is allowed to practice medicine provided they display *Scottulaejnir* on their door, which loosely translates as 'Quack Doctor'.

... it was once illegal to own a pet dog in Reykjavik.

... anyone caught trespassing can be fined 1/400th of a dollar.

In India ...

... long ago a fiancé was required to deflower his future bride if she died before the wedding. The girl could not be cremated until this ritual was carried out in front of the village priest.

... children as young as 15 years old can be jailed for cheating in their final examinations in Bangladesh.

... amongst the Malagasy tribe if a son is taller than his father, then the father has to pay his son either in money or give him an ox.

… nude bathing is banned even in the holiday resort of Goa.

… at one time there was a law that forbade lower caste people from casting their shadows on people of higher castes.

… because it is believed that carrot seeds have contraceptive qualities, women in the Indian state of Rajastan are encouraged to eat them.

In Iran …

… the law in Iran suggests that sex play between men and wild animals is not recommended, especially when it involves a lioness.

… there are more than 100 offences that carry the death penalty in Iran.

… it is forbidden to eat snakes on a Sunday.

In Israel ...

... if a pig owner wishes to kill his pig, he is legally obliged to do so himself.

... it is illegal to pick one's nose on the Sabbath.

... in the city of Arad it is considered an offence to operate a neuter clinic, as it is regarded as peddling.

... in the same city feeding animals in public places is strictly against the law.

... no person is allowed to dress or undress in a room with the light switched on.

... there is no legal way for any man named Cohen to marry a divorced woman.

... it is forbidden to bring bears on to the beaches in Haifa.

... pork cannot be legally sold.

... Bicycles may not ridden without a license.

... a law that has now been repealed stated that an illegal radio station that had been maintained for five or more years would become legal.

In Italy ...

... in Milan people are legally required to smile at all times, although there are exemptions for patients in hospitals, or those attending funerals.

... it is illegal to make coffins out of anything other than wood or nutshells.

... in Naples a man is allowed to have as many mistresses as he wishes, provided that his wife knows, and that he can afford to maintain his wife and mistress in the lifestyle to which they are accustomed.

... it is illegal to take photographs out of airport windows.

... you can be arrested after paying for your drinks and food in any Italian café, if you do not pick up your receipt and take it at least 40 metres away from the café.

... on entry to the Vatican, you can be ejected if your clothes are not suitable.

... in the 16th and 17th centuries the amount prostitutes could charge depended on how high their heels were. As a result a law was passed prohibiting women from wearing high heels.

... men can be arrested for wearing skirts.

In Japan ...

... it is illegal to wear the colour purple unless you are mourning the dead.

... in ancient times any Japanese citizen who attempted to leave the homeland was liable to be put to death. However, in 1630, in order to curb emigration the government banned the building of large ocean-going ships.

... there are several driving offences. Pedestrians always have the right of way and there is a zero-tolerance policy on drink driving (this also applies to bicycles).

In Laos ...

... women are not allowed to show their toes in public.

In Madagascar ...

... it is illegal for pregnant women to wear hats.

In Malaysia ...

... it is illegal for Malaysian restaurant owners to substitute a table napkin with toilet paper.

In Mexico ...

... in Guadalajara it is illegal to shout offensive words in any public place.

... women who work for the government of the city of Guadalajara may not wear miniskirts or any other 'provocative' garment during office hours.

... in 1932, in the state of Vera Cruz, priests were banned as citizens.

... an old law which became obsolete in 1963 made it illegal for anyone to be out on the public streets in Tepatitlan Jalisco after the hour of 11pm without their spouse or unless they were working.

In New Zealand ...

... the legal age for drinking is 20, but if you are married and have just turned 18, you can drink in the pub so long as you are with your spouse. However, if you don't have your spouse with you, you have to be 20!

... if you are in a relationship with someone for over three years and decide to split then there is a 50/50 property divide. In some cases, when there are children and in other circumstances, this law may affect relationhips of under three years.

In Paraguay ...

... if a man catches his wife in bed with somebody else he is legally entitled to kill his wife and her lover, but only if he acts immediately.

... duelling is legal, provided both parties are registered blood donors.

In Peru ...

... the use of chilli sauce and similar hot spices added to prison food is outlawed. These items are thought to be aphrodisiacs and therefore unsuitable for pent-up inmates.

... sodomy has long been a serious offence. A person who has engaged in this act is dragged through the streets on a rope. Hanging comes next before the corpse is burned, fully clothed. This is said to symbolise the sodomite's total destruction.

... unmarried young men are prohibited from having a female alpaca live in their homes or apartments.

In Russia ...

... it is illegal to drive a dirty car.

STAP ME, BORIS, HAVE YOU SEEN THE DUST ON THESE WHEEL ARCHES?

… the police were once allowed to 'beat peeping toms soundly'.

… an old law stated that if a train approached a citizen sleeping on the tracks, it had to stop and wait until the citizen had finished his rest.

... during the reign of Catherine I, the rules for parties stipulated that no man was to get drunk before 9 o'clock and women weren't allowed to get drunk at any hour.

... during the time of Peter the Great any Russian who wore a beard was required by law to pay a special tax.

In Qatar ...

... all foms contraception are strictly forbidden because Qatar needs more males to work and more females to bear and raise children.

... if an unmarried woman becomes pregnant she is prohibited from using any hospital in the region, or from calling for any medical assistance. Her only options are either to do without health care or leave the country.

... in Doha, if a man surprises a naked Muslim woman while bathing or dressing she must first cover her face, not her body.

In San Salvador ...

... drunk drivers can be punished by death before a firing squad.

In Saudi Arabia ...

... in 1979 women were banned by royal decree from using the hotel swimming pools in Jeddah.

... it is against the law for a woman to appear in public without a male relative or guardian present.

... women are not allowed to drive cars.

... the importation of any books featuring Christian symbols, such as a cross, is illegal.

... should an infidel accompany a Muslim then both are required to use the highways for infidels.

... under no circumstances can any contraception be brought into the country. Anyone caught smuggling birth control pills, condoms, or other contraceptive devices can expect to receive a 6-month prison sentence.

... adulterers are punished by being tied into a cloth sack and then stoned to death, or alternatively the woman is shot in front of her lover, who is then publicly beheaded.

... it is illegal to engage in any religious practice other than Islam.

grounds for divorce...

... a wife can divorce her husband if he fails to keep her supplied with coffee.

... male doctors may not examine women and female doctors cannot examine men.

In Singapore ...

... chewing gum on public transport systems is regarded as 'a means of tainting an environment free of dirt' and is punishable by a fine or a prison sentence.

... smoking, spitting, and feeding birds in public places are all civic crimes and incur instant fines.

... urinating in a lift is considered a civic crime.

… failure to flush a public toilet is punishable by a fine or prison sentence if you are caught by the special police, who conduct random checks.

… if you are caught littering the streets more than three times the penalty is to clean the streets on Sundays while wearing a bib proclaiming 'I am a litterer'. This will then be broadcast on the local news.

In South Korea ...

… traffic police are legally obliged to report all bribes offered by motorists.

In Spain ...

… in the 18th century an attempt to ban the sombrero caused one Prime Minister to be banished after the ensuing rebellion was quelled.

In Swaziland ...

… in 1985 it was made illegal to have sex at Kadl-Padl hot springs, as the tourist hot spot had also become a popular place for couples to act out their sexual fantasies. The penalty was up to one year in jail.

In Sweden ...

… it is illegal for parents to shame or insult their children.

… it is legal for Swedes to go into photo booths and take topless photos. But full frontal photos are illegal.

… it is illegal to train a seal to balance a ball on its nose.

In Switzerland ...

… the Sabbath is vigorously upheld, and on Sundays people may not wash their cars, hang out their clothes to dry, or mow their lawns, because it causes too much noise and risks drowning out the sound of church bells.

… it was once illegal to flush the toilet after 10pm if you lived in a flat.

… it was once illegal to slam your car door shut.

… every citizen is required by law to have a bomb shelter or access to a bomb shelter.

In Syria …

… a man is forbidden to look at the body of a woman who is not his wife.

In Thailand …

… when a man is driving he must always wear a shirt.

… throwing chewed gum down on the pavement incurs a heavy fine. Failure to pay the fine simply results in a jail sentence.

… it is illegal to step on any Thai money out of respect to their Royal Family, since all currency has the image of the King printed on it.

… it is illegal to leave your house if you are not wearing underwear.

Tonga ...

... going shirtless in public is a punishable offence.

Turkey ...

... all drivers in Turkey must carry a hygienic body-bag suitable for transporting a corpse weighing up to 18st 12lb (120 kilos), or else face a fine and up to 6 months in jail.

... in the 16th and 17th centuries anyone caught drinking coffee was put to death.

... women can be fined up to one quarter of their salaries for appearing in public without having their heads covered. To sidestep this law women in central Turkey's Islamic strongholds wear wigs in hospitals and state offices.

... it is an offence to insult the Turkish nation or the national flag, or to vandalise or tear up the national currency.

In the UAE ...

... in Abu Dhabi, the police can arrest a person for 'committing an action that would be harmful to the general public'. Something as innocent as a man kissing a woman on her cheek in a public place would incur a penalty of ten days in jail for both parties.

United States ...
In Alabama ...

... bogies may not be flicked in the wind.

... it is illegal to wear a fake moustache that causes laughter in church.

... impersonation of a minister of any religion is prohibited by state law.

In Alaska ...

... stern penalties exist for allowing huskies inside school buildings.

... looking at a moose from the window of an aeroplane is illegal.

... feeding alcohol to a moose is an offence.

In Arkansas ...

... flirting between women and men on the streets of Little Rock can result in a 30-day jail sentence.

… you may not keep an alligator in your bathtub.

… if you live in Little Rock and your dog barks after 6pm you can be fined.

… after 9pm it is illegal for a person to sound the horn on a vehicle in any location where sandwiches or cold drinks are served.

… a law decrees that schoolteachers who bob their hair will not get a raise in salary.

In Arizona …

… if caught stealing citrus fruit in Yuma you may be administered castor oil as a punishment.

In California …

… the Paitue Indian reservation laws forbid a mother-in-law to spend more than 30 days a year with her children.

… cats and dogs have to be licenced before having sex.

… no animal is allowed to mate publicly within 500 feet of a tavern, school or place of worship.

… according to the Recruitment Code of the US Navy anyone 'bearing an obscene and indecent' tattoo will be rejected.

… in Riverside it is illegal to kiss unless both people have wiped their lips with rose water.

… in Pacific Grove it is a misdemeanour to kill a butterfly.

… a law created in 1925 prohibits women from wiggling their bottoms while dancing.

… women cannot drive cars while dressed in a housecoat.

… it is an offence to detain a homing pigeon.

… in Covina a husband is not guilty of deserting his wife if she rents a room to a boarder and therefore crowds him out of the house.

In Los Angeles …

… you cannot bathe two babies in the same bathtub at the same time.

… it is illegal for a customer at a meat market to poke a turkey to see how tender it is.

... it is forbidden to hunt moths under a streetlight.

... babies are forbidden to ride alongside food in supermarket trolleys.

In San Francisco ...

... picking up used confetti and throwing it is banned.

... if walking an elephant down Market Street it must be kept on a leash.

… it is illegal to clean one's car with used underwear.

… playing poker in public or gambling in a barricaded room is illegal.

In Colorado …

… it is against the law in Pueblo to allow a dandelion to grow within the city limits.

… in Gunnison it is illegal for a man to either hide his wife's lipstick or to throw it away.

… it is a crime for a teacher or professor to fail grading the son or daughter of a fireman in Glenwood County.

In Denver

… the dogcatcher must notify dogs of their impending impoundment by posting notices on trees and along a public road running through the city park.

… be kind to rats, it is illegal to mistreat them.

… it is illegal to lend your vacuum cleaner to your next-door neighbour.

In Connecticut ...

... restaurant owners are required to provide separate nose-blowing and non nose-blowing sections in their restaurants.

... a local ordinance bans people in Woodville from playing Scrabble while waiting for a politician to speak.

... in order for a pickle to be officially called a pickle it must bounce.

In Dakota ...

... in Pine Ride it is illegal for a dog to 'snarl in an unfriendly manner' at pizza delivery boys.

... in Bismark, North Dakota, every home within the city limits must have a hitching post for a horse in the front yard.

... if you lie down and fall asleep with your shoes on in North Dakota, you are committing a crime.

... in any bar, restaurant or club it is illegal to serve beer and pretzels at the same time.

In Delaware ...

... every minor used to have to inform his or her parents before engaging in sexual intercourse.

... unless carrying sufficient supplies of drink and food, it is illegal to fly over any body of water.

In Florida ...

... it is illegal to put livestock on board a school bus.

... it is illegal to get a fish drunk.

... you and the salon owner can both be fined if you fall asleep under the hair dryer at the hairdresser.

... if you try to commit suicide and do not succeed, you are free. However, if you do succeed it is a felony and you can be jailed.

... farting in a public place after 6pm on Thursdays is illegal.

... it is illegal for women to expose more than two thirds of her bottom at the beach. If the bikini doesn't cover at least one third of her rear end a $500 fine can be imposed.

... it is illegal for a train to pass through Gainesville at a faster speed than a man can walk.

... in Key West turtle racing is not allowed within the city limits.

In Georgia ...

... it is illegal for unmarried couples to have sexual intercourse.

... it is illegal for a barber to advertise his prices.

... it is illegal to spread false rumours.

... it is illegal in Gwinnett County for residents to keep rabbits as pets. The county livestock law restricts rabbits to farm areas and homes where there is at least three acres of land for the animals to roam.

... it is illegal to slap a man on the back or front.

... it is illegal to be caught swimming in the nude anywhere in the vicinity of Georgetown. Offenders are transported to the outskirts of town and left to fend for themselves. And if they partake in any sexual activity whilst skinny dipping, they are covered with paint, attached to an ass and transported out of the town where they are left and told never to return.

In Hawaii ...

... owning a snake of any kind is illegal, with the exception of zoos, who are allowed to have two provided that they are both male and non-venomous.

BUTCH & MELVIN

... to be seen in public wearing only swimming trunks and little else is an act of indecency.

... it is illegal to own a mongoose without a permit.

... within the city parks of Honolulu, it is unlawful to annoy birds.

... in Honoluluit is illegal for any woman to be on Waikiki Beach or in the water without wearing 'modesty shoes' or 'lightweight bathing footwear'.

In Idaho ...

...anti-delinquency statutes prohibit juveniles from deliberately stepping on ants.

... in East Bancroft Ville County it is illegal to wake a sleeping city alderman.

... in the town of Idaho Falls anyone aged over 88 is forbidden to ride a motorcycle.

... any police officer in Coeur d'Alene who suspects that sex is taking place somewhere must always drive up from behind, honk their horn three times, and then wait two minutes before getting out of their vehicle to investigate.

'You gotta help me quick, Sheriff —
the sausages come off in 6 minutes!'

… you cannot buy onions after dark without a special permit from the Sheriff.

In Illinois …

… it is legally stipulated that a car must be driven with the steering wheel.

… barbers are banned from using their fingers to apply shaving cream to a patron's face.

… if visiting a theatre in Winnetka it is illegal to remove your shoes if your feet smell.

… animals can be sent to jail. A monkey served five days in a Chicago jail for shoplifting.

… monkeys were banned from smoking cigarettes in South Bend, Indiana.

… all bachelors should be called master, not mister when addressed by women.

… it is against the law to eavesdrop.

… plying a dog with alcohol is illegal.

In Chicago ...

... it is forbidden to eat in a place that is on fire.

... a hat pin is legally regarded as being a concealed weapon.

... it is illegal to take a French poodle to the opera.

In Iowa ...

... kisses may last no more than five minutes.

... Fort Madison firemen are required to practice for 15 minutes prior to attending to a fire.

In Kansas ...

... it is illegal to wash your false teeth in a public drinking fountain in McLough.

... in Wichita a man's mistreatment of his mother-in-law may not be used as grounds for divorce.

... when two trains approach one another at a crossing, they must both stop and neither is allowed to start up again until the other has gone.

... catching fish with one's bare hands is illegal.

… on the city streets of Lawrence, a law bans anyone from carrying bees in their hat.

… state law requires pedestrians on the highways at night to wear tail lights.

… in Russell it is against the law to have a musical car horn.

In Kentucky …

… law requires every citizen to take a bath at least once a year.

… men who push their wives out of bed for inflicting their cold toes on them can be fined or jailed for a week.

… it is illegal for a merchant to force a person into his place of business for the purpose of making a sale.

… the law states that a person is considered sober until he or she can no longer stand.

… it is legal for a wife to put castor oil in her husband's drink (to keep him from drinking).

… in Owensborough no woman may buy a new hat without her husband first trying it on.

… marrying the same man four times is illegal.

In Louisiana …

… a bill was once instigated in the State House of Representatives that fixed a ceiling on the price of haircuts for bald men at 25 cents.

… biting someone with your natural teeth is 'simple assault' while biting someone with false teeth is 'aggravated assault'.

… gargling is prohibited.

… it is illegal to rob a bank and then shoot at the bank teller with a water pistol.

In Maryland …

… a woman may not go through her husband's pockets while he is sleeping.

… it is illegal to mistreat an oyster.

… no matter how dirty they get, it is illegal to wash sinks in Baltimore.

… the song *Short People* by Randy Newman is banned on the radio.

In Massachusets ...

... it is illegal to take more than two baths a month within the confines of the city of Boston.

... it is illegal to post an advertisement on a public urinal in Boston.

... a state law forbids cooling one's feet by hanging them out of the window.

... mourners may not eat more than three sandwiches at a wake after attending a funeral.

... it is illegal to shave whilst driving.

... it is illegal to have a goatee beard unless you first pay a special licence fee for the privilege of wearing one in public.

... snoring is strictly forbidden unless all bedroom windows are closed and securely locked.

... it is illegal to deface milk cartons.

In Michigan ...

... the law states that anyone bathing in public in Rochester must have their bathing suit inspected by a police officer.

... married couples must live together or face imprisonment.

... it is against the law for a lady to lift her skirt more than 6 inches while walking through a mud puddle.

... a woman is not allowed to cut her hair without the permission of her husband.

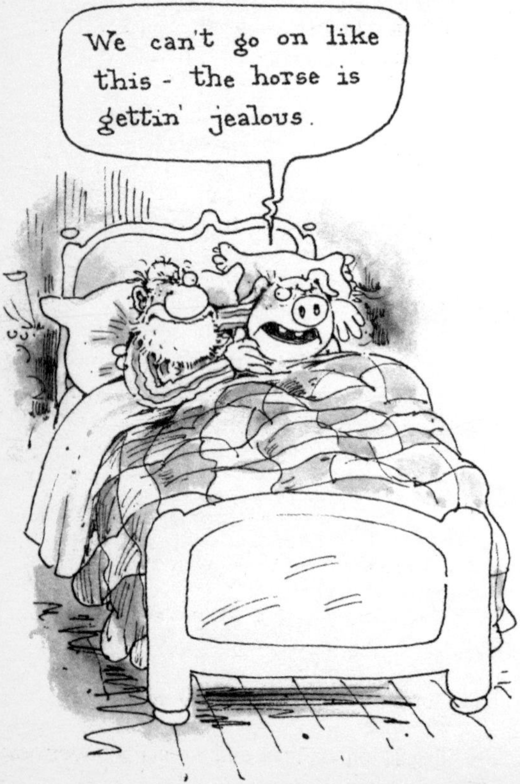
We can't go on like this - the horse is gettin' jealous.

… dentists are officially classed as 'mechanics'.

… in Clawson a farmer can legally sleep with his pigs, cows, horses, goats and chickens.

In Detroit …

… children must abide by certain laws or else their parents can be jailed. Children under 18 must not play truant from school, be found on the streets after a set curfew, or be seen associating with juvenile delinquents.

… couples are banned from making love in a car unless the act takes place while the vehicle is parked on the couple's own property.

… it is illegal to loiter in the city morgue.

In Minnesota …

… in Brainerd every man is required to grow a beard.

… a tax form asks for your date of death.

… it is illegal to hang men and women's underwear on the same washing line.

... selling a car or making too much noise on the Sabbath could put you in jail for a month of Sundays.

... teasing skunks is illegal.

In Missouri ...

... a man must have a permit to shave.

... in Moberley it is illegal to gulp loudly while drinking water, or to sniff or blow your nose in public.

... women are prohibited from wearing corsets in Merryville because, 'the privilege of admiring the curvaceous, unencumbered body of a young women should not be denied to the normal, red-blooded American male'.

... it is illegal for an off-duty fireman to rescue a woman who is only wearing a nightgown. In order for her to be rescued she must be fully clothed.

... women in Saco are forbidden from wearing hats that might frighten timid persons, children or animals.

In Nebraska ...

... a parent can be arrested if his or her child cannot hold back a burp during a church service.

... without holding a state license it is illegal for a mother to give her daughter a perm.

... the owner of every hotel in this state is required to provide each guest with a clean and pressed nightshirt. No couple, even if they are married, may sleep together in the nude or have sex unless wearing one of these clean, cotton nightshirts.

... spitting into the wind is illegal.

... it is a crime for a wife to open her husband's mail.

... it is unlawful to eat fried chicken while walking down the sidewalk.

In Nevada ...

... until the 1960s it was illegal to sell alcohol at religious camp meetings, within half a mile of the state prison, in the State Capitol Building, or to imbeciles.

... in Las Vegas is against the law to pawn your dentures.

... it is illegal to drive a camel on the highway.

... spiteful gossip defined as 'talking behind someone's back, without cause' or 'unwarranted gossip' is illegal.

In New Jersey ...

... slurping soup in a public place is illegal.

... courting couples in Liberty Corner must refrain from sexual intercourse in parked cars as they can face jail terms, especially if the car horn is inadvertently sounded during the act.

... unless you have a written note from your doctor it is illegal to buy ice cream after 6pm.

... cabbage cannot be sold on a Sunday.

... in Willingsborough it is illegal to display a 'for sale' sign outside your house.

... in some towns garage sales are banned ... unless the house is up for sale.

In New Mexico ...

... during lunch breaks in Carlsbad no couple should engage in a sexual act whilst parked in their vehicle, unless the car is equipped with a curtain.

... in Quemado a newspaper can be fined if it misspells a person's name in print.

... it is illegal for women to pump gas. Instead, men must willingly volunteer to pump for single women. The same rule applies to flat tyres.

... females are prohibited from appearing in public unshaven.

In New York ...

... it is illegal to use more than one seat on the subway.

... it is against the law for children to pick up or collect cigarette and cigar butts.

... it is illegal to start any kind of public performance, show, play or game until after 1.05pm.

... at one time, any man caught turning around on any city street and flirting with a woman was fined $25. Should the same man be convicted twice of the same crime then he would be forced to wear a 'pair of horse-blinders' wherever and whenever he went outside for a stroll.

... jaywalking is legal, as long as it's not diagonal. That is, you can cross a street at right angles to the sidewalk, but you can't cross it diagonally.

… it is unlawful for any person to do anything that is against the law. (!)

In North Carolina …

… a law was once passed making it illegal for a rabbit to run down the street.

… it is still illegal for people to buy and sell labelled milk crates as they were often used as items of furniture.

… if an unmarried man and woman go to a hotel or motel and register themselves as 'Mr and Mrs' then according to state law they are legally husband and wife.

… all couples staying overnight in a hotel must have a room with double beds with a distance of at least two feet between them. Making love in the space between the beds is not allowed.

… massage parlours are banned in Hornytown

… South Carolina state law forbids crawling around in public sewers without a permit.

In Ohio ...

... if you wish to keep a bear you must have a licence.

... a 1995 city ordinance in Sandusky outlawed trick or treating by anyone older than 14.

... a law was passed banning women from wearing patent leather shoes in Cleveland in case a man might catch a glimpse of something he shouldn't.

... in Oxford, it is illegal for a woman to strip in front of a man's picture.

In Oklahoma ...

... it is illegal to make ugly faces at a dog.

But I always look like this!

… it is illegal for a baseball team to hit the ball over the fence or out of the ballpark.

… it is a felony to bite someone else's hamburger.

… laughing at a joke made by a lawyer is illegal.

In Oregon …

… in Grant's Pass you can throw onions at 'obnoxious salesmen' if they won't stop knocking on your door or ringing your doorbell.

… in Salem it is illegal for patrons of establishments that feature nude dancing to be within two feet of the dancers.

… wearing 'puke green' coloured socks on a Sunday is prohibited under the Oregon State Constitution.

… in Hood River, juggling is not permitted without a licence.

… before entering the Pacific Ocean, swimmers must remove their socks.

… in Willowdale men can be fined for using profane language during intercourse with their wives. Their wives can say what they like.

In Pennsylvania ...

... singing in the bath was once illegal.

... in Harrisburg it is illegal to have sex with a truck driver in a tollbooth.

... a special cleaning ordinance bans housewives from concealing dirt and dust under a rug in a dwelling.

... no man may purchase alcohol without written consent from his wife.

... ministers are forbidden to marry a couple if either is drunk.

... many years ago the Farmer's Anti Automobile Society proposed some 'rules for the road'. Firstly, automobiles travelling on country roads at night had to send up a rocket every mile, and then wait for ten minutes for the road to clear before proceeding. Secondly, if a driver saw a team of horses, he was to pull to one side of the road and cover his vehicle with a dust cover that had been painted to blend into the scenery. Thirdly, in the event that a horse refused to pass a car on the road the owner had to take his car apart and conceal the parts in the bushes.

… all counties must provide veterans' graves each year with a flag, most of which are distributed before Memorial Day.

… it is illegal for over sixteen women to live in a house together since this is thought to constitute a brothel. Yet up to 120 men can live together without breaking the law.

In Rhode Island …

… jumping off bridges in Providence is against the law.

… it is illegal to sell toothbrushes on Sunday.

… it is illegal for farmers to plant corn in March.

In Tennessee …

… the sale of bologna (sandwich meat) is prohibited on Sundays.

… it is illegal to give any pie to fellow diners, as it is to take any uneaten pie home in a doggie bag. Law stipulates all pie must be eaten on the premises.

… women are not allowed to call a man for a date.

...shooting any game other than whales from a
moving automobile is illegal.

...frogs are banned from croaking after 11pm in
Memphis.

...in Monique Pass, it is a felony to allow a dog to
eat a child's homework.

...you are not allowed to sell hollow logs.

... it is a felony in Harrity to carry a concealed rain
gauge without permission.

In Texas ...

... in Galveston it is illegal to have a camel run loose in the street.

... the law requires criminals to give their victims 24 hours notice, either orally or in writing explaining the nature of the crime to be committed, before committing the crime.

... in Clarendon lawyers must accept eggs, chickens or other produce (as well as money) as payment of legal fees.

Same as you said, JB — I'd never regret having to shell out on a good lawyer!

… men over 50 years old, and one-eyed men are exempt from peeping tom charges.

… it is against the law to graffiti someone else's cow.

… in Alamo a person found intoxicated must be administered a large dose of castor oil by a local doctor – failure to gulp it down will result in a fine.

… some years ago a city council member in Albuquerque proposed a resolution to ban Santa Claus from the city.

… it is still a hanging offence to steal cattle.

… in Abilene loitering or idling anywhere within the confines of the city for the purposes of flirting is illegal.

In Utah …

… a man is held responsible for every criminal act committed by his wife in his presence.

… in Salt Lake City it is unlawful to carry an unwrapped ukulele in the street.

... swearing in front of a dead person is illegal.

... a law makes it a crime to curse on a bus.

... daylight must be visible between dancing couples.

... birds have the right of way on the highways.

In Vermont ...

... women must obtain written permission from their husbands in order to wear false teeth.

... it used to be law that everyone had to take at least one bath each week on a Saturday night.

... whistling under water is illegal

... denying the existence of God is illegal.

In Virginia ...

... chickens must lay eggs between 8am and 4pm, not before or after.

... the Code of 1930 has a statute that bans corrupt practises or bribery by any person other than political candidates.

... a man in Norfolk can face 60 days in jail for patting a woman's bottom.

... it is illegal to flip a coin in a restaurant in Richmond to determine who pays for a meal, as this is considered a form of gambling.

... in Lebanon it is illegal for husbands to kick their wives out of bed.

... in Norfolk there used to be a men-only job in the civil service for a corset inspector, because it was illegal for women to go out without wearing a corset.

... it is illegal to drop a dead fish into someone's bathing suit in Buckroe Beach.

In Washington ...

... it is against the law to pretend that one's parents being rich.

... it is illegal to sleep in an outhouse without the owner's permission.

... any restroom with pay toilets must have an equal number of free toilets. This law came into effect as a result of the speaker of the State House of Representatives racing to an all-pay facility without any money.

... it is illegal to catch a fish by throwing a rock at it.

... you are allowed to transport an aquarium on public transport buses so long as the fish remain still.

... you are not allowed to carry a concealed weapon that is over 6 feet in length.

In West Virginia ...

... you can be imprisoned for cooking cabbage or sauerkraut due to the horrendous smell.

… in Romboch it is illegal to engage in sexual activity with the lights on.

… only babies are allowed to ride in a baby carriage.

… no members of the clergy are allowed to tell jokes or humorous anecdotes from the pulpit whilst conducting church services.

In Wyoming …

… the state once passed a law making it illegal to spit on the sidewalks or in the streets in front of a lady. Anyone who offended a lady by doing so was arrested and jailed for three days, after which restitution had to be paid.

… in Newcastle couples are banned from having sex while standing inside a store's walk-in meat freezer.

… in Rock Springs it is illegal for flying instructors to place their arms around a woman without a good and lawful reason.

Miscellaneous American Statutes

Under Illinois law, it is a violation to build a snowman taller than 10 feet (3 metres).

In Tryon, North Carolina, it is illegal for anyone to keep 'fowl that shall cackle' or for anyone to play the piccolo between the hours of 11pm and 7.30am.

In certain cities that have designated themselves as 'Stress Free Zones', stress is illegal. Anybody seen under stress in these places must be given a free ice cream bar.

In some states of the USA nudity is illegal.

It is a crime to fall asleep while wearing a fur coat under the Washington State Constitution.